# Wasps
# For Kids

# Amazing Animal Books
# For Young Readers

By
Rachel Smith

*Mendon Cottage Books*
***JD-Biz Corp Publishing***

**All Rights Reserved.**

No part of this publication may be reproduced in any form or by any means, including scanning, photocopying, or otherwise without prior written permission from JD-Biz Corp

Copyright © 2015. All Images Licensed by Fotolia and 123RF.

Read More Amazing Animal Books

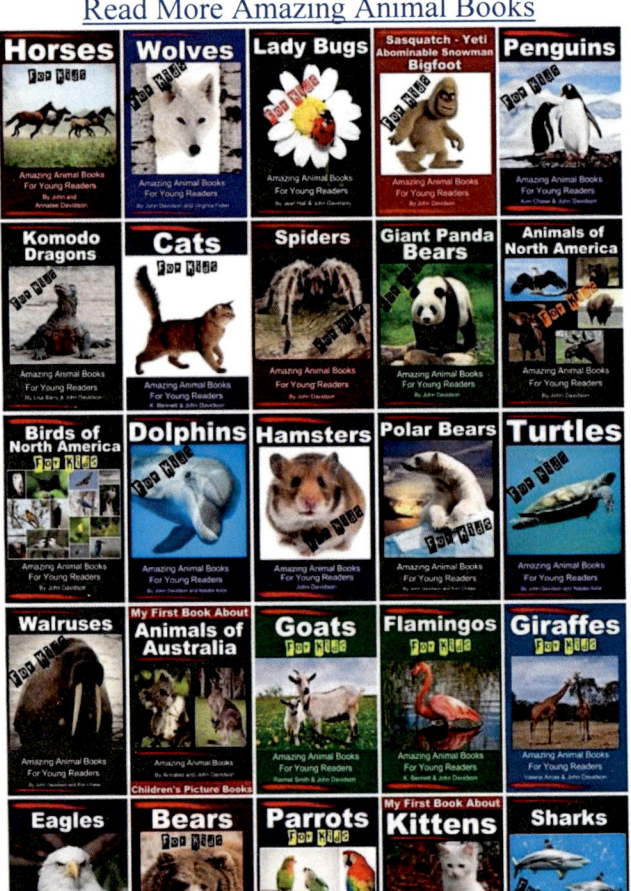

Purchase at Amazon.com

# Table of Contents

Introduction .................................................................................................. 4

What is a wasp? ........................................................................................... 5

What kinds of wasps are there? ................................................................. 9

The history of wasps and humans ............................................................ 12

Yellow jacket .............................................................................................. 16

Hornet ........................................................................................................ 19

Fig wasp ..................................................................................................... 21

Conclusion ................................................................................................. 23

Author Bio ................................................................................................. 24

# Introduction

Wasps are an insect most people know about and hate very much. At the same time, they know very little about them except that they can sting more than one time, and some kinds are kind of cranky.

With most of them having the telltale yellow and black stripes, people know to steer clear of wasps. Yet, they don't have these colors just to warn people; there's more to the wasp's coloring than that. And many of them have entirely different coloring too, such as the green hornet.

Most are familiar with the common wasp, but there are so many different kinds of wasps that there's no hope of including a good description of all of them even in a thousand page book.

Some are small, some are huge. Some reproduce in different ways; others pollinate plants, and others don't. There's an incredible amount to know about the wasp and all its kinds.

So, read on, and discover the things they never tell you about wasps.

# What is a wasp?

The term wasp is a wide net to cast. It basically means any insect in the suborder Apocrita that is not an ant or a bee. This means that sometimes it can be a little fuzzy as to what is a wasp and what is not, and how they are all related. Some people prefer to stick with a close family related to the common wasp; others consider wide differences between wasps. Whatever the case, the wasp family is huge.

A wasp building part of a nest.

Most of the wasps that American and Canadian folks think of are wasps such as hornets and yellow jackets. These kinds of wasps are called eusocial, which means that they live in communities together and don't fight each other. Other types of wasps, the majority of them, actually, are solitary. This means they live alone.

It's believed that ants, bees, and wasps all come from the same ancestor many hundreds of thousands of years ago or more. This is why they're in the same order.

Wasps can be anywhere from 12.5 centimeters to 0.2 millimeters, depending on the species. There are tens of thousands of known species, meaning that there may be more wasps in places like dense jungle that we don't even know about yet. There are still so many animals undiscovered in places like that; the world is not done being explored.

Many other bugs tend to copy the look of the wasp. This is called Batesian mimicry, meaning they look alike to protect themselves. These bugs can't sting, but predators believe they can because they look like wasps. This is sometimes done with bees too.

Wasps lay eggs, though their ways of doing it vary from species to species. Wasps first become larvae, then become pupae, then grow up to become full grown wasps. A larva is a small, wormish sort of creature. A caterpillar, for example, is a larva, and ants also have larvae. Most wasp larvae look like maggots, and they are need a protected environment, as they can't survive in their own without either a safe place to grow up or that plus a mother feeding them.

Pupae are mostly grown babies, but they are not adults yet.

Sex is determined by the mother. If she wants female babies, she fertilizes them; she only needs to mate with a male at any time, and she can use it any time afterward. A fertilized egg become a female; an unfertilized egg becomes a male. In many wasp types, female born of the same mother are very close genetically.

Wasp mothers that feed their babies tend to do only that. Other than providing food, a wasp mother has no obligation to her babies, and will not really do anything else for them. However, the babies generally only need a food source, and they can grow and then figure out the rest on their own.

Interestingly, in some cases, wasps feed on their own larvae's salivary secretions (basically spit). The spit is very nutrient rich and especially has protein, something the wasp can't get on its own.

Wasps have three parts to their body: the head, the mesosoma, and the metasoma. The head is pretty obvious, as most creatures have heads, but what are the mesosoma and the metasoma?

The mesosoma is the thorax (chest sort of area) and the first bit of the abdomen. It is attached to the metasoma by the petiole, a skinny waist that has been the basis for what is called a 'waspish figure.'

The metasoma is the abdomen. It's the part that has the stinger, as well as other body parts.

A wasp necessarily as an insect has an exoskeleton. An exoskeleton is a hard covering that holds in the body parts inside. Unlike humans, who have a skeleton inside their bodies to hold them together, the exoskeleton is on the outside and there are no bones in an insect body. Instead, it's pretty much all goo.

Wasps also have membranous wings. A membrane is a thin material stretched over something. Humans have many membranes in their bodies, though they aren't made out of the same things as the membranes in wasp wings. The wings are held together by small hooks.

Female wasps in some species don't have wings.

Wasps also have large compound eyes. This means they have multiple areas they look out of their eyes, which gives them better vision than humans. They also have several simple eyes, more like a human's, arranged in a triangle on their forehead. These are called ocelli.

Like grasshoppers, wasps have mandibles that can bit and cut. Mandibles are a kind of mouth thing, but a bit different from a human mouth, since they're nearly so flexible or soft as human lips or a human mouth. The big difference between most wasps and grasshoppers and other insects is that the wasp has a proboscis. This is a long sort of tube thing that it uses to suck up nectar.

# What kinds of wasps are there?

There are many different kinds of wasps, as you know, but there are several classifications (groups they're sorted into). Here are a few of them.

A green hornet.

Parasitoids are wasps that lay their eggs in other larva or insects. These are usually creatures such as caterpillars. Parasitoids may paralyze the host, leaving it to be eaten alive by the larvae. Some lay their eggs inside the host, some just put them on the outside. But whatever way they do it, it is not a pleasant end for the host.

These kinds are usually solitary wasps. This makes sense because solitary wasps don't build nests, so they need somewhere protected to put their young. It is definitely kind of gross, but the insect world is not a forgiving one.

Social wasps, on the other hand, tend to lay their eggs in their nest. The nest is built out of what we call paper. It has a lot in common with human paper: it's made out of wood fibers too, and is pretty thin and easy to destroy. However, it's not advised to destroy it, because wasps get pretty angry when they're threatened in such a way.

The eggs are cared for in the nest, and the babies develop there without a need for brutally killing a host. Social wasps's nests tend to have combs like bees, but they don't make honey. It's simply for the babies.

Some wasps are pollinators. This means that, like bees, they help plants spread their pollen and fertilize their seeds so that they can continue reproducing.

Some solitary wasps will live together, but unlike social wasps, they don't work together or divide the labor. Each wasp is responsible for their own offspring, and they have their own space as well.

Some types of wasps are what are called kleptoparasites. These are usually solitary type wasps, and what it means is that they lay their eggs in other wasps' nests. This is similar to what some birds do, except that the larvae don't harm the other larvae.

Some kinds of kleptoparasitic wasps do harm the other eggs or larvae. Sometimes, they even get rid of the original eggs and replace them with their own so that the wasp mother will not even realize she is caring for babies that aren't her own. Sometimes they put them in a paralyzed host that has already had eggs implanted, and the larvae that emerge eat both the host and the other larvae.

If you haven't already guessed it, the phrase should not be 'dog eat dog world.' It should be 'bug eat bug world.'

Another type of wasp is the predator. While there are many wasps who drink nectar as a food, many other wasps are predators. They will generally drink the juices of other bugs, sometimes the eggs or pupae of other bugs especially. Sometimes, they look like they're chewing on them, but they are simply making an opening to suck out the juices.

Wasps can also be prey. There are bee-eaters, which are a kind of bird, and rather than just eating bees, they eat any stinging insect. Another kind is the honey buzzard, which eats wasp larvae. It's the only predator of the Asian giant hornet, a pretty dangerous bug. Said hornet is known also as a 'yak-killer.'

Many kinds of wasps eat nectar, but some also eat fruit and other dead insects (not insects they killed themselves).

# The history of wasps and humans

Wasps and humans don't seem like a good match. In fact, most people tend to either be afraid of wasps, or dislike them greatly. The good thing to know is that wasps won't usually sting unless they perceive a human as aggressive. This includes trying to kill them.

A wasp on a human hand.

However, there is still plenty of good when it comes to the wasp, at least for humans.

Wasps that are parasitoid (that lay their eggs in other insects) are often employed as a natural pest control. How does this work? Well, certain kinds of wasps tend to use certain kinds of insects for their egg-laying. The ones that are used for pest control particularly go after the bugs that are attacking the plant, such as sugarcane or tomatoes.

A rugby team called Wasps RFC is in England. It seems that when it was named, it was very popular to name teams after insects. This was back in the 19th century when this team was created. Unsurprisingly, they make use of the black and yellow stripes.

Wasps have also influenced fashion. For one thing, in especially the 19th century, jewelry with figures of them on them have been popular. In that time period, they were known as wasp brooches.

Another way they seemed to influence fashion in the 19th century was in the use of the 'waspish' figure. This was when a woman would have an itty bitty waist (like a wasp) and wider bust (chest area) and hips. It was actually a somewhat harmful look achieved with tight corsets, often made out of things such as whale bone.

Wasps have also been used in literature, as early as the comedy play by Aristophanes in Ancient Greece. The play was called *The Wasps*, though it was more of a cheeky name for the old jurors who made up the chorus. The chorus in an Ancient Greek play sang certain parts of the show.

Another way wasps have been used in literature is in sci-fi. For example, H. G. Wells used giant wasps in one of his books which had three inch stingers.

One more sci-fi novel, called *Wasp*, uses the idea of how a wasp, despite being tiny, can cause big problems. For example, a wasp can cause someone to really mess up what they're doing, whether it's using a table saw or driving a car, just by being there and frightening them. It's a political kind of book, written in 1957.

Interestingly, Charles Darwin, the father of Evolutionary Theory, said that the parasitoidal wasp was one of the reasons that he didn't believe in a God. To him, the fact that there was such a creature who had its young eat a caterpillar or the like from the inside out while it was still alive could not have been created by a loving god.

The wasp is also commonly a name for military equipment. A lot of ships, in both the British Navy as early as 1749 and in the American Navy, were named *Wasp*. The Germans used the name for a howitzer (a weapon that shoots things a distance, kind of like a cannon), and the British used it for a flamethrower and a helicopter.

Wide Angle Search for Planets, which is also called WASP, has given its name to many planets, though it's not really related to the wasp, but rather a sort of coincidence that they have the same name.

Wasps do not exist in every part of the world. For instance, the Faroe Islands did not have wasps until fairly recently, when turf for soccer (or football) was brought over from Denmark and accidentally brought over a number of wasps. These wasps are more aggressive than normal wasps. This is because they are used to warmer air, and cold air makes wasps both cranky and more desperate to survive. It's no wonder, since they can't leave somewhere like the Faroe Islands, which are far from other shores!

# Yellow jacket

The yellow jacket is a black and yellow creature, except when it's red, black, and yellow. Yellow jacket is the term in North America for a number of wasps that live in that area. In places like Europe, they may simply be called wasps.

A yellow jacket collecting pollen and nectar.

Yellow jackets tend to have distinctive markings; these aren't just stripes, but often have a triangular-looking part to the stripes as well. As mentioned before, most yellow jackets are black and yellow, but a few are red, black, and yellow.

Sometimes, yellow jackets are mistaken for bees. While they are related, they are definitely a group of wasps. The mistake is easy to make with the black and yellow ones, though. They are also mixed up easily with other wasps, such as hornets and paper wasps. This, again, is mainly due to coloring and size.

Yellow jackets are eusocial, so that means they live together in a group. There are worker yellow jackets, which get food and build the nest, and then there's the queen and the drones.

The interesting thing about the yellow jacket is that all the workers are female, and they are unable to reproduce. The queen is of course female as well, though she can reproduce. Queens lay eggs for workers, drones, and other future queens. Drones are all male and are only used for reproducing.

The way it works is this: the queen is a young queen that has fertilized eggs from her mother's nest. She survives the winter hidden away, and then, when it's warm enough, comes out and builds a small nest and lays eggs in it. These eggs are mostly worker bees, but she has to feed them all until they grow enough to work.

When the nest is big and has thousands of worker bees, this is around the time that a queen lays eggs that will become queens themselves, and she also has the drones to fertilize their eggs. Then, she dies in the fall (or autumn), and the new queen bees hide in the winter until they get their chance to have their own nest.

Yellow jackets have barbed stingers. Typically, unlike the honey bee, their stingers do not come off when they sting someone, and they will sting repeatedly. Sometimes, however, the stinger does come off and the yellow jacket dies.

Their stingers have venom, but it's typically harmless to humans unless they are allergic or stung a large number of times.

These types of wasps usually only last a season or so. However, in some warmer climates that have mild winters, they do a thing called overwintering, which means they survive the winter and continue to grow their nests and populations. This can lead to an enormous nest with multiple queens.

# Hornet

Hornets have a lot of similarities to yellow jackets. Their reproduction is the same for the most part, and they have queens, drones, and worker wasps.

A Japanese giant hornet.

Drones have what they call a nuptial flight. They fly out in mid-autumn (or fall) to find queens to mate with, and then die shortly after. The drone does not help build the nest, find food, or anything of the sort. Their only job is to mate with queens so that they can start a nest in the spring.

A hornet's head is a light shade of orange, though its antennae are a slightly different color.

Hornets have more painful stings than most wasps. This is because they have more of a certain chemical in them.

The European hornet is the most well known. Despite its name, it actually lives in not only Europe, but also Asia and North America. The hornet doesn't live below the Northern Hemisphere, which means the top half of the world.

The Asian giant hornet is an interesting one. It is the largest kind of hornet, and it is known by locals as the yak-killer hornet. In Japan, it's known to be an enemy of the local honey bees, though they have a special technique to kill it. The Japanese giant hornet can only stand a body temperature a couple degrees lower than a Japanese honey bee can, and so the honey bees, which are much smaller than the hornet, will cluster on it and heat it up until it dies.

This type of hornet also uses food recruitment signals. It's one of the only ones that does this. This means that the hornets that live together use signals to bring them along to sources of food.

Female hornets, workers, look exactly like queens, but smaller. Drones look very similar too, but they don't have stingers.

# Fig wasp

'Fig wasp' can refer to two kinds of wasps belonging to the same family: parasitoid wasps and pollinating wasps. There are various sorts belonging to each kind, but that's a simple way of looking at it.

Wasp pollinating a flower.

Interestingly, these two kinds are actually at odds.

Pollinating fig wasps are in a mutualistic relationship (a relationship where both sides are helped) with certain fig trees. The way these fig trees' flowers are pollinated is like so:

A fertilized female climbs into a flower/starting to develop fig through a special hole. It has to fight its way in, often ripping off its antennae and wings to get in. Then it lays its eggs in the seed sort of area. Then it dies.

The seeds become larvae and grow up in the fig. Then, the males, who never grow wings, mate with the females and dig them a hole out. Then the males die.

And the whole cycle starts over again.

With the parasitoidal or non-pollinating wasp, it's a bit different. Unlike the pollinating wasp, which puts pollen in the flower when it crawls up it, the other wasp bores into the fig and implants its eggs there. Its babies will eat the pollinating wasp's babies.

With the parasitoidal wasp, the females are the ones who never leave the fig. The males are the ones who leave, and they mate with females.

# Conclusion

Wasps are fascinating creatures that often live brutal lives. It's very tough in the insect world, and the wasp manages to pull out ahead a lot of the time.

From the Asian giant hornet, which strikes terror into the hearts of its victims, to the pollinating fig wasp that helps the fig tree in a mutualistic relationship, the world of wasps is varied and interesting.

There are thousands upon thousands of wasps in the world, and they help more than they hinder. They are pest removers in a natural way, they are inspiration to artists and other creators, and they even help pollinate some plants.

Wasps are a boon, and they are here to stay.

# Author Bio

Rachel Smith is a young author who enjoys animals. Once, she had a rabbit which was very nervous, and chewed through her leash and tried to escape. She's also had several pet mice, which were the funniest little animals to watch. She lives in Ohio with her family and writes in her spare time.

Our books are available at
1. Amazon.com
2. Barnes and Noble
3. Itunes
4. Kobo
5. Smashwords
6. Google Play Books

JD-Biz Corp

P O Box 374

Mendon, Utah 84325

http://www.jd-biz.com/

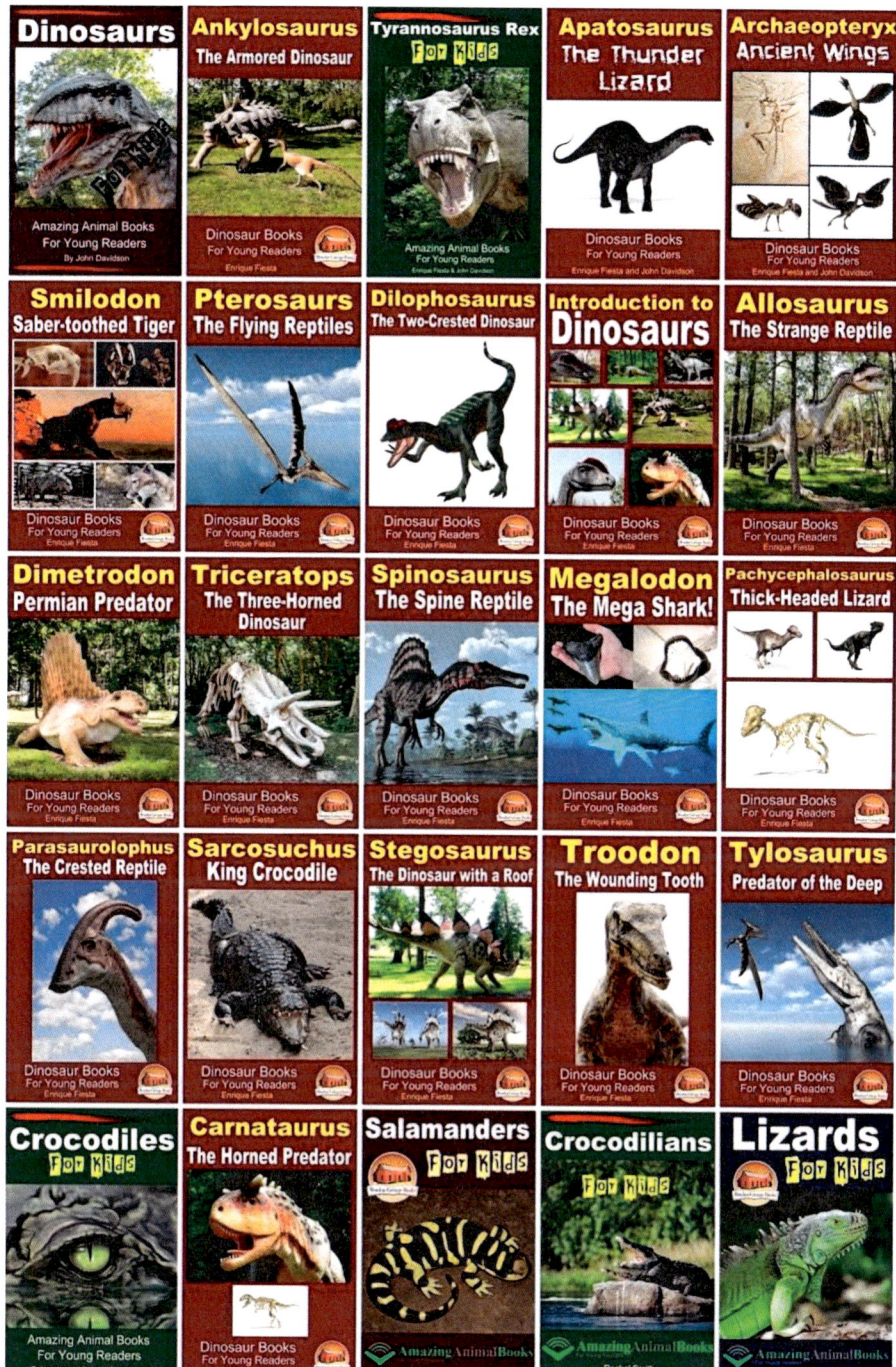

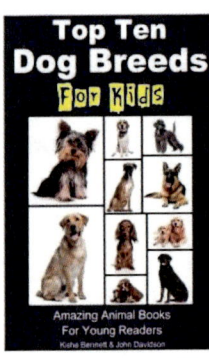

Made in United States
North Haven, CT
04 March 2022